Spatial Computing

Harnessing the Future of AR, VR, and Digital Integration

Taylor Royce

Copyright © 2024 Taylor Royce

All rights reserved.

DEDICATION

The vision and inventiveness of the pioneers and creators of spatial computing, whose work continues to push the limits of technology and human experience, are honored in this book. To the scientists, engineers, designers, and visionaries who have dedicated their lives to making spatial computing a reality and creating a future in which the digital and physical realms coexist together.

I hope that this work will honor your achievements and act as a manual for the upcoming generation of artists, builders, and thinkers. I dedicate this book to the people who will keep pushing the boundaries of spatial computing and encouraging us all to think about what else might be possible.

DISCLAIMER

This book's content is solely intended for general informative purposes. Even though every attempt has been taken to guarantee the content's accuracy and dependability, the author offers no guarantees or assurances about the information's timeliness, accuracy, or completeness. The author's ideas and viewpoints are their own, and they may not represent those of any institutions, businesses, or organizations that are referenced.

When using any of the methods, resources, or suggestions described in this book, the reader should use their own judgment. Any negative effects, including but not limited to monetary, professional, or personal ones, that may result from the use or abuse of the material supplied are not the author's responsibility.

This book may contain links, external websites, or references to other sources. Including such references does not mean that the information in those sources is approved or that the author is responsible for it. Before drawing conclusions from the information in this book, readers are urged to independently confirm any facts.

Spatial computing is a quickly changing field, and when new developments and technology appear, the material presented may become out of date.

CONTENTS

ACKNOWLEDGMENTS 1

CHAPTER 1 1

Comprehending Spatial Computing 1

   1.1 What Spatial Computing Is and How It Started 1

   1.2 Essential Elements of Spatial Computing 3

   1.3 Using AI to Improve Spatial Awareness 5

CHAPTER 2 8

The technologies that underpin spatial computing 8

   2.1 AR, or augmented reality 8

   2.2 VR, or virtual reality 10

   2.3 MR, or Mixed Reality 13

CHAPTER 3 16

Spatial Computing's Business Applications 16

   3.1 Improving Remote Work and Collaboration 16

   3.2 Use Cases in Manufacturing and Industry 18

   3.3 Retail and Interaction with Customers 21

CHAPTER 4 25

Spatial Computing and Healthcare 25

   4.1 Simulation and Training in Medicine 25

   4.2 Medical Attention and Therapy 28

   4.3 Management and Infrastructure in Healthcare 30

CHAPTER 5 34

Spatial Computing Education and Training 34

    5.1 Revolutionizing Education in the Classroom....................... 34

    5.2 Professional and Corporate Education............................... 37

    5.3 Research and Higher Education...................................... 39

CHAPTER 6..42

Gaming and Entertainment..42

    6.1 Immersive Video Games.. 42

    6.2 Production of Film and Media....................................... 45

    6.3 Interactive Media's Future... 47

CHAPTER 7..51

Real Estate, Architecture, and Design...................................51

    7.1 Design and Visualization of Architecture....................... 51

    7.2 Sales and Marketing of Real Estate................................ 54

    7.3 Smart Cities and Urban Planning....................................56

CHAPTER 8..60

Defense and Security Applications of Spatial Computing.....60

    8.1 Simulation and Training for the Military....................... 60

    8.2 Protection and Monitoring... 63

    8.3 Response and Recovery to Disasters.............................. 65

CHAPTER 9..69

Difficulties and Moral Issues..69

    9.1 Security of Data and Privacy... 69

    9.2 Inclusivity and Accessibility.. 72

    9.3 Financial and Technical Obstacles................................. 74

CHAPTER 10..77

Spatial Computing's Future.. 77

10.1 New Developments and Trends... 77
10.2 Forecasts for the Upcoming Ten Years... 80
10.3 Getting Ready for a Future in Space...82
ABOUT THE AUTHOR..85

ACKNOWLEDGMENTS

From the bottom of my heart, I want to thank everyone who helped make this book possible. First and foremost, I want to express my gratitude to the pioneers and innovators in the field of spatial computing, whose contributions have influenced and molded the concepts discussed here. Their commitment to technological advancement keeps expanding the realm of what is conceivable.

I would especially like to thank my mentors, coworkers, and industry professionals who so kindly offered their knowledge, experience, and insightful criticism with me during the writing process. Your advice has been crucial in helping to shape this book into what it is now.

I want to express my gratitude to my family and friends for their constant encouragement and support. Your confidence in me has consistently inspired me.

Lastly, I want to thank the readers, both those who are new to this profession and those who have already embraced it. My goal is for this book to be a helpful tool that encourages you to investigate the countless opportunities that spatial computing presents.

Without everyone's combined work and contributions, this book would not have been possible. Thank you.

CHAPTER 1

COMPREHENDING SPATIAL COMPUTING

1.1 What Spatial Computing Is and How It Started

Transformation from Simple Computer Interfaces to Immersion Environments

From conventional 2D interfaces to dynamic, immersive environments that combine the real and virtual worlds, spatial computing signifies a radical change in how people engage with technology. Punch cards and text-based user interfaces were the mainstays of early computers. With the development of graphical user interfaces (GUIs), users were able to visually interact with digital systems. Building on these pillars, spatial computing transports users to settings where the virtual and real worlds coexist together.

The first head-mounted display (HMD), created by Ivan Sutherland in 1968, set the stage for augmented and virtual reality systems. This is one of the major turning points in the development of spatial technologies.

- The 1990s saw the development of AR technologies like Boeing's AR-based assembly guide and the introduction of virtual reality (VR) headsets like the Sega VR.
- The 2010s saw the widespread use of smartphones, which made it possible for AR and VR to reach large audiences with devices like the Oculus Rift and apps like Pokémon GO.
- The current day is: Spatial computing is now widely used in fields including healthcare, gaming, and urban planning thanks to developments in AI, computer vision, and the Internet of Things.

How the Digital and Physical Worlds Are Integrated by Spatial Computing

Real-time overlaying of digital data or objects on top of physical spaces is how spatial computing works. Devices with sensors, cameras, and processors that record the surroundings and create interactive digital layers enable this integration. For instance, augmented reality apps overlay data or images on the real world using the cameras on smartphones.

- VR systems produce completely virtual worlds that aren't related to real-world locations.
- Real-time engagement is made possible by mixed reality (MR), which combines digital and physical components.

1.2 Essential Elements of Spatial Computing

Virtual Reality (VR) and Augmented Reality (AR)

- **AR, or augmented reality:** By superimposing digital components like text, pictures, or 3D models, augmented reality (AR) improves the physical world. Applications include AR-enabled shopping apps that allow customers to "try on" items virtually and navigation systems that show directions onto a windshield.
- **Virtual reality, or VR:** Virtual reality (VR) produces vivid virtual worlds that completely replace the real world. VR is frequently experienced by users through headgear, and it has uses in employee training simulations, gaming, and virtual

travel.

Both Extended Reality (XR) and Mixed Reality (MR) are included. By enabling users to manipulate digital things in real-world settings, MR goes beyond AR. Engineering fields like architecture and manufacturing are being revolutionized by devices like Microsoft's HoloLens, which allow engineers to design and interact with prototypes in real-time.

XR (Extended Reality): XR is a catch-all word that includes AR, VR, and MR. It highlights the smooth transition between the physical and virtual worlds, spurring advancements in entertainment, healthcare, and education.

Computer vision, IoT (Internet of Things), and sensor technology

- **Sensor technology:** Sensors record environmental information, including motion, temperature, and spatial dimensions, allowing for accurate mapping and interaction. LiDAR scanners and depth cameras are two examples.
- **Vision of Computers:** Computer vision, a fundamental component of spatial computing,

analyzes visual information to identify objects, monitor motion, and comprehend surroundings. This helps autonomous cars identify impediments and drive safely.
- The Internet of Things (IoT) enhances spatial computing systems by forming interconnected networks of devices that share data. The Internet of Things' function in spatial computing, where sensors and gadgets interact to improve living conditions, is best illustrated by smart homes.

1.3 Using AI to Improve Spatial Awareness

The Function of AI and Machine Learning in Spatial Computing

Large datasets are analyzed by AI algorithms to enhance spatial systems' comprehension of their surroundings. AI-powered augmented reality applications, for example, are able to identify landmarks and give users up-to-date navigational or historical data. Similar to this, robotics uses AI to give machines spatial awareness so they can move around and communicate on their own.

Interaction with the Environment and Real-Time Data Processing

Real-time data processing and response is one of the most attractive aspects of spatial computing. For instance:

- **Gaming:** AI-driven non-playable characters (NPCs) in virtual reality settings respond to user movements to produce dynamic and captivating experiences.
- **Healthcare:** Surgeons use AI-enhanced real-time imaging technologies to execute minimally invasive procedures with previously unheard-of accuracy.

Intelligent environments and predictive modeling

Machine learning is used by spatial computing systems to forecast future events and enhance interactions. Important instances consist of:

- **Urban Planning:** To create safer and more effective urban areas, AI models model traffic patterns for cars and pedestrians.
- **Store:** By examining consumer behavior and making necessary adjustments to digital displays or recommendations, intelligent environments customize the retail experience.

Spatial computing, which combines AI and IoT with AR, VR, MR, and XR technologies to create dynamic, intelligent systems, represents a paradigm shift in the way humans and machines interact. From improving workplace productivity to transforming healthcare, entertainment, and other sectors, this discipline has the potential to revolutionize a wide range of businesses. Spatial computing redefines what is possible in the environment and alters our perception of it by fusing the digital and physical domains.

CHAPTER 2

THE TECHNOLOGIES THAT UNDERPIN SPATIAL COMPUTING

2.1 AR, or augmented reality

Superimposing Digital Data on the Physical World

Through the overlaying of digital elements including text, graphics, and interactive features, Augmented Reality (AR) improves the user's experience of the real environment. AR smoothly incorporates these digital components into real-world situations, as contrast to VR, which transports viewers to wholly virtual environments. Devices with cameras, sensors, and computers that can map the world in real time are how augmented reality works.

- For instance: When a smartphone AR app, such as Google Lens, is directed at an object or text, it can recognize landmarks, translate words, or offer contextual information.
- Because of its adaptability, augmented reality (AR) is useful in a variety of fields, including

entertainment (like Pokémon GO) and industrial applications like superimposing maintenance instructions on equipment.

Key AR Applications and Devices
- **Healthcare:** To increase accuracy during procedures, surgeons utilize AR to see anatomical features in three dimensions.
- **Retail:** AR applications let buyers see furniture in their homes or "try on" clothes before making a purchase.
- **Education:** Students find difficult subjects like biology or physics more interesting and understandable when they participate in interactive augmented reality experiences.

Devices:
- **HoloLens:** Microsoft's augmented reality headset is extensively utilized in industrial design and training.
- **AR-Enabled Smartphones:** AR is made accessible to the general public through gadgets like iPhones and Android phones that have the ARKit or ARCore frameworks installed.

Difficulties in AR Development

- **Hardware Restrictions:** AR devices must strike a compromise between portability and long battery life and computing power.
- **Environmental Variability:** Robust environmental mapping is necessary for effective augmented reality experiences, yet it can be disturbed by cluttered surroundings, reflective surfaces, or inadequate lighting.
- **User Experience:** Creating AR interfaces that are easy to use and accessible is still difficult, particularly for non-technical people.

The cost of developing advanced augmented reality applications and technology is high, making them inaccessible to smaller companies or underfunded industries.

2.2 VR, or virtual reality

Building Completely Immersive Digital Worlds

By immersing users in fully computer-generated surroundings, virtual reality (VR) allows for experiences that range from fantasy worlds to realistic simulations. In contrast to AR, VR uses head-mounted displays (HMDs) and other sensory devices to fully replace the user's actual environment.

Applications:

- **Gaming**: Virtual reality provides an unmatched degree of immersion, enabling gamers to engage with games more deeply.
- **Training:** To provide safe, realistic training environments, industries such as aviation and medical use virtual reality simulations.
- **treatment:** VR provides patients with controlled situations in exposure treatment, which is used to treat PTSD and phobias.

Well-known VR Platforms and Sectors Using VR Platforms:

- **Oculus (Meta):** Celebrated for its stand-alone Quest gadgets, Oculus has transformed reachable virtual reality experiences.
- **HTC Vive:** Offers realistic virtual reality experiences appropriate for business use.
- **PlayStation VR:** Allows console players to experience virtual reality.

- **Healthcare:** VR-based rehabilitation programs help stroke victims with their motor skills.
- Virtual property tours enable prospective purchasers to virtually inspect locations in real estate.
- **Education:** VR classrooms, especially for STEM areas, make learning dynamic and interesting.

Advances in VR Hardware and Software
Hardware:
- **Displays:** Wider fields of view and higher resolution improve realism.
- The use of haptics devices, like gloves and suits, enhances immersion by providing physical feedback.
- Motion tracking guarantees accurate and responsive interactions in virtual environments.

Software:
- **Graphics Engines:** Visually appealing virtual reality environments are powered by engines such as Unreal and Unity.
- **AI Integration:** AI makes it possible for VR to have adaptive learning experiences and realistic NPC behavior.
- **5G and Edge Computing:** Higher data rates and

lower latency enhance virtual reality streaming and multiplayer functionality.

2.3 MR, or Mixed Reality

Creating Interactive Experiences by Combining AR and VR

In order to create settings where digital and actual items coexist and interact, Mixed Reality (MR) combines aspects of AR and VR. MR allows real-time interaction with digital elements integrated into the physical world, as opposed to AR, which mainly overlays information, and VR, which isolates people in digital domains.

- For instance: Virtual participants in an MR-enabled meeting can interact with physical items like whiteboards while appearing as holograms in a real-world conference room.

Use Cases in Gaming, Education, and Healthcare

- **Gaming:** By facilitating player interaction with real-world items (such a table), MR enables the creation of hybrid gaming experiences.
- **Education:** Using MR, students can investigate

difficult subjects by seeing and interacting with real classroom objects while exploring a virtual molecule.

- **Healthcare:** Surgeons can work with a virtual 3D representation of a patient's anatomy in conjunction with real-world data when using MR for pre-operative planning.

Differences Between MR and Traditional AR/VR

- **Interaction Depth:** While AR concentrates on superimposing data and VR isolates users in virtual worlds, MR stresses interactivity by enabling users to control digital items in real-world settings.
- **Hardware:** MR frequently calls for sophisticated headgear with hand-tracking and spatial mapping features, such as Microsoft's HoloLens or Magic Leap.
- **Complexity of Application:** Strong AI and computer vision systems for smooth integration, as well as knowledge of both AR and VR technologies, are necessary for creating MR solutions.

The combination of AR, VR, and MR technologies is

largely responsible for the transformational potential of spatial computing. Each has a distinct influence on how people engage with both digital and real-world surroundings. Advances in hardware, software, and innovative applications across industries are propelling these technologies' further evolution, indicating a future in which spatial computing will play a crucial role in daily life.

CHAPTER 3

SPATIAL COMPUTING'S BUSINESS APPLICATIONS

3.1 Improving Remote Work and Collaboration

Online Spaces for Collaboration

Through the creation of virtual spaces that allow people to communicate as if they were in the same room, spatial computing is revolutionizing team collaboration. By adding spatial presence and interactive 3D components, these areas go beyond conventional video conferencing solutions.

- **Immersive Meetings:** With platforms like Spatial or Meta's Horizon Workrooms, teams can work together in real time, manipulate models, and see projects in three dimensions.
- **Cross-Disciplinary Collaboration:** Managers, engineers, and designers may easily share ideas, which minimizes the misunderstandings that come with more conventional communication techniques.

Advantages:
- Lowers expenses by eliminating the need for in-person travel.
- Enables teams that are spread out geographically to participate equally, promoting inclusion.

Digital Twins for Project Visualization

Organizations may view, evaluate, and optimize projects in real time with the help of digital twins, which are virtual copies of physical assets.

Use Cases:
- **Construction:** Before a single brick is laid, stakeholders can take a virtual tour of construction models.
- **Urban Planning:** Digital twins are used by cities such as Singapore to model and plan the growth of their infrastructure.
- **Product Design:** Without building physical models, designers can virtually iterate prototypes to find problems.

Benefits:
- Quickens the decision-making process.
- By modeling possible situations, predictive analytics

is improved.

By superimposing instructions or guidance into a worker's range of vision, Augmented Reality (AR) allows for real-time remote assistance.

Instances in Action:
- **Field Service:** AR glasses can provide a technician troubleshooting machinery with step-by-step instructions, minimizing downtime.
- **Medical Field:** Using augmented reality to highlight important locations, surgeons can confer with distant specialists during procedures.
- **Customer Support:** Complex product users can interact with professionals who offer guidance, increasing user happiness.

Impact:
- Increases productivity and lowers error rates.
- Knowledge transfer is facilitated, especially in sectors with aging labor forces.

3.2 Use Cases in Manufacturing and Industry

AR-Assisted Repair and Maintenance

Through AR, spatial computing has transformed equipment maintenance by offering real-time, context-aware assistance.

How It Works:
- Technicians can overlay maintenance instructions, operating data, or schematics over machines using augmented reality devices.
- Interactive, step-by-step instructions are provided by systems such as PTC's Vuforia, which even highlights sections that need to be maintained.

Benefits:
- By giving precise, contextually appropriate information, it reduces errors.
- It lowers the amount of training new hires need.
- Improves operating efficiency by expediting repair times.

VR Simulations for Training Employees

Employees can study and practice skills in safe, regulated environments created by virtual reality (VR).

Applications:
- **Hazardous Industries:** Employees in industries such as oil and gas can rehearse emergency

procedures without being exposed to real dangers.
- **Equipment Training:** By virtually acquainting themselves with intricate machinery, operators can reduce the likelihood of mistakes during real-world operation.
- **Soft Skills Development:** Virtual reality is used to teach managers or customer service representatives how to handle difficult interpersonal situations.

Advantages:
- By providing engaging, hands-on training, retention rates are raised.
- It lowers the price of actual training facilities.
- Training is easily scalable, enabling a worldwide workforce to access it.

Spatial Computing in Logistics and Supply Chain Management

Through improved efficiency, visibility, and predictive capabilities, spatial computing offers substantial advantages to the logistics industry.

Key Applications:
- **Warehouse Management:** By superimposing instructions, AR headsets help employees pick

things quickly.
- The most effective delivery routes can be planned and simulated with the use of digital twins of supply networks.
- Accuracy is increased through real-time products monitoring made possible by the combination of IoT and spatial computing in inventory tracking.

Impact:
- Lowers operating expenses through waste reduction and increased accuracy.
- Decision-making is improved by using real-time insights.

3.3 Retail and Interaction with Customers

AR-Driven Shopping Experiences

By combining the digital and physical shopping experiences, augmented reality is revolutionizing the retail industry.

In-Store Experiences:
- Customers can scan products using augmented reality to see comprehensive details, reviews, or suggestions.

- Customers can try on clothing or accessories virtually in fitting rooms without actually wearing them.

Incorporation Online:
- With AR apps, consumers can see how cosmetics will look on their skin or how furniture will look in their houses.

Instances:
- Customers may digitally test goods with Sephora's augmented reality cosmetics app.
- IKEA Place uses augmented reality to assist consumers see how furniture should be arranged.

Advantages:
- Increases client trust, which lowers return rates.
- Increases conversion rates by improving engagement.

Product Visualization and Virtual Showrooms
- Customers can explore and interact with products in completely immersive virtual reality shopping settings.
- Automobile manufacturers such as Audi employ virtual reality (VR) to display automobile models so

that buyers can experience the features and interiors.
- Virtual tours of houses are provided by real estate companies, allowing purchasers to view homes from a distance.

Benefits:
- Increases reach by removing regional restrictions.
- It eliminates the requirement for actual display areas or inventories.

Enhanced Customer Service Through Spatial Interfaces

By utilizing immersive interfaces, spatial computing opens the door to a new era of customer service.

- **Chatbots and AI-Driven AR:** Smart AR interfaces give customers immediate replies to their questions while offering visual guidance.
- **In-Store Navigation:** Augmented reality applications direct shoppers to merchandise or offer detailed directions for self-checkout.
- **Personalized Experiences:** By combining AI and location computing, retailers may provide customized suggestions, resulting in more enjoyable shopping experiences.

The outcomes are as follows:

- Enhanced client loyalty and satisfaction.
- Simplified processes with less reliance on human labor.

From improving teamwork and optimizing industrial processes to revolutionizing retail experiences, spatial computing is propelling innovation in a variety of sectors. Its capacity to merge the digital and physical realms is opening up previously unheard-of efficiency and economic opportunities. The future of labor, commerce, and engagement will be shaped by the technology's rapidly growing impact on business applications.

CHAPTER 4

SPATIAL COMPUTING AND HEALTHCARE

By incorporating cutting-edge technologies like augmented reality (AR), virtual reality (VR), and artificial intelligence (AI) into patient care, medical education, and infrastructure management, spatial computing is completely changing the healthcare industry. This chapter examines the revolutionary uses of spatial computing in healthcare, emphasizing how it can enhance patient and practitioner experiences, save costs, and improve outcomes.

4.1 Simulation and Training in Medicine

Surgical Simulations Using Virtual Reality

With its immersive and risk-free surroundings for practicing intricate procedures, virtual reality (VR) is revolutionizing the way surgeons train.

Applications:

- **Simulated Operations:** With the help of VR

systems such as Osso VR, trainees may carry out intricate surgical procedures while receiving realistic feedback that replicates the textures and resistance of human tissue.
- In order to improve synchronization for difficult surgeries, teams might practice working together virtually during training.

Benefits:
- By enabling repeated practice without the use of cadavers, it improves skill development.
- Because trainees are more confident and precise when they enter operating rooms, there are less mistakes made during actual procedures.
- Enables access to top-notch surgical training worldwide.

Augmented Reality (AR) for Anatomy Education
- AR gives students a multi-layered, interactive understanding of human anatomy.

How It Operates:
- AR programs such as HoloAnatomy project 3D human body models onto real-world locations, enabling students to closely examine organs,

muscles, and bones.
- By rotating, zooming, and dissecting virtual models, users can better comprehend anatomical linkages.

Impact:
- Enhances accessibility and engagement of learning.
- Aids in bridging the gap between practical application and theoretical understanding.

Emergency Response Team Training
- For emergency response teams to be ready to address crises like mass casualty events or natural disasters, spatial computing is essential.

Uses:
- Virtual reality scenarios assist teams practice resource allocation and triage by simulating stressful events like multi-car accidents.
- AR tools improve situational awareness by offering real-time assistance during training.

Advantages:
- Enhances preparedness for unforeseen crises.
- It lessens the possibility of errors in real-world situations.
- Enhances group decision-making and

communication under duress.

4.2 Medical Attention and Therapy

AR-Guided Diagnostics and Procedures

Through the direct overlay of critical information onto the patient or surgical field, augmented reality is improving surgical precision and diagnostic accuracy.

Applicability:

- AR in Surgery: During procedures, surgeons can see interior structures in three dimensions thanks to devices like Microsoft HoloLens, which improves accuracy and reduces invasiveness.
- The ability of AR systems to analyze imaging data (such as CT scans) in real-time and provide detailed overlays to guide diagnosis is known as "Enhanced Diagnostics."

Advantages:

- Enhances surgical results and lowers complications.
- It makes minimally invasive operations possible, which reduces recovery times.

VR Therapy for Rehabilitation and Pain Management

By immersing patients in therapeutic situations, virtual reality is proven to be a useful tool for pain management and recovery.

Applications:

- **Pain Management:** By engrossing patients in soothing virtual environments, virtual reality diverts them from painful procedures, such burn treatments.
- **Rehabilitation Physical:** By gamifying rehabilitation exercises, platforms such as MindMaze encourage patients to follow their treatment regimens.

Benefits:

- Decreases dependence on opioids and other painkillers.
- Increases participation and adherence to rehabilitative initiatives.
- Enhances mental well-being by lowering stress and anxiety.

Spatial computing enhances remote consultations

Through the creation of immersive telemedicine experiences, spatial computing helps close the distance between patients and medical professionals.

Features:
- **3D Visualization:** During virtual consultations, doctors can describe symptoms and treatment plans using 3D models.
- **Home Care AR Support:** Real-time instructions for utilizing medical devices or giving medication can be obtained by patients via AR-enabled devices.

Impact:
- Increases healthcare access in underserved or remote locations.
- Shortens patient wait times and travel expenses.
- It makes remote diagnostics more accurate.

4.3 Management and Infrastructure in Healthcare

Digital Twin Technology for Hospital Planning

By providing virtual representations of medical facilities, digital twins facilitate effective management and planning.

Applications:
- **Facility Design:** Prior to construction, planners can forecast bottlenecks, optimize layouts, and simulate operations.
- **Operational Efficiency:** To improve hospital

operations, digital twins track data in real time, such as patient flow or equipment usage.

Benefits:
- Early detection of inefficiencies lowers expenses.
- By allocating resources optimally, it improves the experiences of both staff and patients.

VR for Treatment of Phobias and Mental Health

With regulated exposure therapy, virtual reality is a new method for treating phobias and mental health issues.

Applications:
- **Phobia Treatment**: Virtual reality settings assist patients in safely and controlledly facing their anxieties, such as those related to heights, spiders, or public speaking.
- **Stress and Anxiety Relief:** Users can reduce stress by immersing themselves in peaceful virtual environments through immersive relaxation programs.
- **PTSD Therapy:** Through VR therapy, veterans and trauma survivors can process and revisit events.

Advantages:
- Therapy is tailored to each patient's needs.

- By providing private and discrete treatment alternatives, it lessens stigma.
- Enhances results by permitting regulated and gradual exposure.

Simplifying Administrative Processes

Healthcare workers' workloads are being lessened by the automation and optimization of administrative duties brought about by spatial computing.

The following are the main improvements:
- **Patient Records Management:** AR overlays make it easier for workers to find and retrieve patient records in an emergency or during consultations.
- **Staff Training and Scheduling:** VR tools enhance scheduling using predictive analytics and offer onboarding simulations.
- **Inventory Management:** Real-time tracking of medical supplies using IoT and spatial computing ensures prompt refilling.

Impact:
- It gives medical professionals more time to devote to patient care.
- Minimizes mistakes in resource allocation and

record-keeping.
- Increases overall effectiveness of operations.

By bringing cutting-edge tools and solutions to patient care, medical education, and infrastructure management, spatial computing is revolutionizing the healthcare industry. More effective, precise, and individualized healthcare experiences are being made possible by its capacity to bridge the gap between the digital and physical worlds. These technologies' influence on the healthcare sector will surely increase as they develop further, influencing a future in which state-of-the-art technology improves human welfare.

CHAPTER 5

SPATIAL COMPUTING EDUCATION AND TRAINING

The delivery of education and training is being redefined by spatial computing, which makes it more engaging, dynamic, and efficient. The incorporation of AR (Augmented Reality), VR (Virtual Reality), and other spatial technologies is generating revolutionary possibilities in both corporate and educational settings. This chapter explores the ways that spatial computing is improving advanced research, professional skill development, and educational experiences.

5.1 Revolutionizing Education in the Classroom

AR Textbooks and Virtual Field Trips
Through the creation of captivating virtual learning environments, spatial computing is enabling students to learn outside of the traditional classroom.
Online Field Trips:

- **How It Operates:** With virtual reality (VR), students can experience remote or inaccessible places like the ocean's depths, historic monuments, or even space.

Instances:

- Lessons become more memorable when professors lead students on immersive tours using platforms like Google Expeditions.

Impact:

- Learning becomes more vivid and experiential.
- Exposure to varied places broadens kids' perceptions.

AR Textbooks:

- By superimposing interactive 3D models and animations on printed materials, augmented reality (AR) makes textbooks come to life.
- For instance, biology students can watch chemical processes happen right on the page or explore the human heart in three dimensions.
- By converting static knowledge into dynamic experiences, these tools promote greater comprehension and involvement.

Enhanced STEM Education with Interactive Models

Spatial computing is revolutionizing STEM (science, technology, engineering, and mathematics) education.

Interactive Simulations:

- Students studying physics can see motion and forces in three dimensions.
- Students of engineering can virtually test their designs and model building structures.

Advantages:

- Encourages experiential learning without requiring costly physical equipment.
- Through the use of visualization, difficult ideas are made understandable to students of all skill levels.

AR Special Needs Education Applications

With its customized tools to serve a range of learning requirements, spatial computing is revolutionizing special education.

Applications:

- AR apps give audible and visual clues to help autistic children comprehend social interactions.
- Virtual reality environments offer secure areas for rehearsing real-world situations, such as shopping or

crossing the street.

Benefits:
- By accommodating different learning methods, it fosters inclusivity.
- It helps kids with special needs become more self-assured and independent.

5.2 Professional and Corporate Education

VR for Safety Training and Skill Development

Particularly in high-stakes situations, virtual reality is an effective tool for professional and corporate training.

Applicability:
- **Skill Development:** Before working on real machinery, engineers and mechanics can practice difficult assembly jobs in virtual reality.
- **Safety Instruction:** By simulating dangerous situations like chemical spills or fire drills, virtual reality (VR) enables staff members to rehearse reactions without the risks of the actual world.

Advantages:
- Lowers expenses related to actual training facilities.
- Reduces the hazards associated with training in

hazardous fields like construction or oil and gas.

AR-Assisted On-the-Job Learning

Augmented reality streamlines the learning process by offering employees real-time direction and assistance.

Instances:
- Technicians can view detailed instructions for repairing machines right in front of them by using AR glasses.
- With AR overlays that display item locations and amounts, warehouse employees may maximize inventory management.

Benefits:
- Minimizes downtime brought on by ignorance.
- Instant access to information improves accuracy and efficiency.

Training Soft Skills in Virtual Environments
- Additionally, interpersonal skills, an area that has historically been difficult to teach, are being developed through the use of spatial computing.

Uses:
- VR simulations assist staff members in honing their

public speaking, conflict resolution, and customer service skills.
- Real-time feedback on tone, body language, and word choice is given by AI-powered avatars.

Advantages:
- Enhances self-assurance in handling practical circumstances.
- Repetitive practice is permitted in a secure, accepting setting.

5.3 Research and Higher Education

Complex Scientific Research Using AR and VR

Exploration and experimentation in science are taking on new dimensions thanks to spatial computing.

Uses:
- Researchers can replicate astrophysical occurrences or see molecular structures via virtual reality.
- Real-time data overlays during experiments are made possible by AR, which facilitates analysis and interpretation.

Impact:
- By allowing academics from all over the world to

engage with the same virtual models, it improves collaboration.
- By providing fresh approaches to data exploration and comprehension, it speeds up discoveries.

Spatial Computing in Engineering and Architectural Design

- AR and VR are essential tools for industries that need careful planning and visualization.

Instances:
- Architects can make real-time alterations while guiding clients through virtual models of buildings.
- Before building starts, engineers can uncover problems by simulating stress testing on virtual structures.

Benefits:
- Minimizes mistakes and expenses related to design modifications.
- Clear, visual project representations facilitate better stakeholder communication.

Online Laboratory for Tests

- Virtual labs are being used by higher education

institutions to increase the affordability and accessibility of experimentation.

How It Works:

- Without the use of tangible objects, students carry out experiments in a simulated setting, such as combining chemicals or testing circuits.
- Instant feedback is provided by virtual labs, which aid students in understanding errors and refining their methods.
- Expands access to high-quality education, particularly in environments with limited resources.
- Enables pupils to freely explore without worrying about safety, which promotes innovation.

Through the creation of more effective, accessible, and engaging learning environments, spatial computing is transforming training and education. The use of AR, VR, and related technologies is changing how we learn and use information, whether it's improving scientific research, improving classroom instruction, or upskilling staff. These tools' influence on training and education will only grow as they develop further, preparing professionals and students for the challenges of the future.

CHAPTER 6

GAMING AND ENTERTAINMENT

By producing immersive, interactive experiences that were previously only found in science fiction, spatial computing is transforming the gaming and entertainment sectors. Technologies like VR (Virtual Reality), AR (Augmented Reality), and AI are influencing the future of interactive storytelling, media production, and gaming by merging the digital and real worlds. This chapter examines these developments and how they affect both consumers and artists.

6.1 Immersive Video Games

VR Gaming Environments
- By immersing gamers in three-dimensional, fully immersive settings, virtual reality has completely changed the gaming experience.
- With the use of VR headgear, hand controllers, and

haptic feedback devices, players are immersed in a virtual environment where they can interact with their surroundings.

- **Physical Interaction:** Players must move, evade, and interact physically with the environment in games like Beat Saber and Half-Life: Alyx.
- **Realism:** Traditional gaming cannot match the impression of realism produced by high-resolution graphics and spatial audio.

The effect on gaming

- VR encourages a greater level of emotional investment and connection with the game.
- With previously unheard-of degrees of immersion, it creates new possibilities for genres like simulation, horror, and adventure.

AR for Mobile and Console Gaming

- Augmented reality creates distinctive gaming experiences that are playable on mobile devices and consoles by fusing digital aspects with the real environment.
- By enabling users to capture virtual monsters in real-world settings, Pokémon GO* popularized

augmented reality.
- Players can create and explore virtual worlds superimposed on their surroundings by playing augmented reality console games like Minecraft Earth.

Benefits:
- Because AR is portable and requires little hardware, a wider audience can use it.
- It encourages participants to explore real-world environments together, which promotes social interaction.

Experiences with Social and Multiplayer Spatial Computing

- Real-time, interactive social experiences made possible by spatial computing have revolutionized multiplayer gaming.

Instances:
- Players can interact, cooperate, and compete in shared virtual environments on VR platforms such as Rec Room and VRChat.
- Players collaborate to find solutions to problems in their local communities using AR games like Harry

Potter: Wizards Unite.
- The social side of gaming is improved by bringing gamers from all over the world together in shared virtual surroundings.
- Enhances the gaming experience by promoting cooperation and teamwork.

6.2 Production of Film and Media

Techniques for Virtual Production
- The production of movies and other media products is being completely transformed by spatial computing.

Virtual Production: What Is It?
- By fusing physical sets with real-time rendering, filmmakers can see scenes as they are being filmed.
- Productions like The Mandalorian, which use virtual backgrounds on LED walls rather than conventional green screens, are powered by tools like Unreal Engine.

Benefits:
- Minimizes the need for location shooting, which lowers production costs.

- Direct integration of effects into filming expedites post-production.
- Enhances creative flexibility by allowing filmmakers to quickly envision and modify sequences.

AR-Enhanced Live Events
- Augmented reality is improving live events and performances by giving viewers engaging experiences.

Uses:
- AR overlays during concerts offer live visual effects that are timed to the music.
- AR is used in sports broadcasts to show virtual replays, player statistics, and game analytics.

Impact:
- Enhances audience participation by giving conventional events more dynamic, engaging layers.
- Attracts tech-savvy audiences seeking out cutting-edge entertainment.

3D Content Creation and Immersive Storytelling
- With the use of interactive tales and 3D content, producers may push the limits of storytelling thanks

to spatial computing.

Instances:

- Through their actions, audiences can shape the tale in interactive virtual reality films like Wolves in the Walls.
- AR apps that combine storytelling and physical engagement, such as *The Line*, transport users to tiny worlds.

Advantages:

- By engaging viewers as active participants in the story, it fosters deeper emotional ties.
- Gives artists fresh resources to try out non-linear narrative and original viewpoints.

6.3 Interactive Media's Future

The Intersection of VR, Film, and Gaming

With the convergence of spatial computing technologies, the lines between interactive media, gaming, and film are becoming increasingly hazy.

New Developments:

- Hybrid experiences, such as Netflix's *Bandersnatch*, blend interactive decision-making

with classic cinema.
- Cross-platform franchises, like Fortnite, include video games, live performances, and movie events all within a single virtual environment.

Implications:
- More interactive, captivating material that combines many forms of entertainment is what audiences are requesting.
- It is imperative for creators to embrace interdisciplinary techniques that integrate technology, game design, and storytelling.

AI-Driven Content Personalization

Artificial intelligence is revolutionizing the way that content is customized to suit the tastes of each individual.
- **Spatial Computing Applications:** AI uses user behavior analysis to suggest storylines or customized gaming experiences.
- Each player has a unique experience thanks to adaptive virtual reality surroundings that vary constantly in response to human inputs.

Benefits:
- By providing customized content, it raises audience

engagement.
- Improves media engagement and game replayability.

Spatial Computing for Online Events and Concerts

The emergence of virtual events demonstrates how spatial computing may be used to produce expansive interactive experiences.

Instances:

- Performers such as Travis Scott and Ariana Grande have drawn millions of fans to their virtual concerts in Fortnite.
- Virtual reality (VR) is being used by platforms such as Wave to offer immersive, surreal concert experiences that transcend physical boundaries.

Impact:

- Making live events available to viewers throughout the world broadens their appeal.
- Promotes creativity in event planning by fusing interactive elements, music, and graphics.

Gaming and entertainment are changing as a result of spatial computing, which opens up new avenues for innovation, engagement, and immersion. It's giving consumers life-changing experiences by fusing the digital and physical worlds, redefining how media is consumed, games are played, and stories are conveyed. A new era of boundless innovation and engagement will be ushered in by the growing influence of technology on entertainment.

CHAPTER 7

REAL ESTATE, ARCHITECTURE, AND DESIGN

Through the introduction of tools and technology that improve visualization, facilitate collaboration, and expedite procedures, spatial computing is revolutionizing the domains of architecture, design, and real estate. These developments revolutionize how experts plan places and interact with clients, from enabling dynamic urban planning to producing incredibly lifelike virtual walkthroughs.

7.1 Design and Visualization of Architecture

AR for Site Planning and Real-Time Adjustments
- By superimposing digital designs onto real-time settings, Augmented Reality (AR) is transforming site planning.
- Architects and planners can use augmented reality (AR) to visualize designs in context by

superimposing blueprints or 3D models onto construction sites.
- On-site design modifications offer instant input and eliminate the need for numerous iterations.

Uses:
- Architects can assess how their designs will blend in with the surroundings by using augmented reality tools such as SketchUp Viewer.
- Developers are able to show stakeholders concepts, guaranteeing agreement on project objectives.

Advantages:
- Facilitates better team collaboration by providing a common visual understanding.
- Early detection of possible spatial conflicts during the design phase lowers errors.

VR Walkthroughs for Design Validation
- Before construction starts, architects and clients can view a design in its entirety using Virtual Reality (VR).
- The ability to completely explore areas and let clients "walk through" their future homes or businesses is one of the benefits of virtual reality

walkthroughs.
- It ensures that design decisions meet expectations by offering insights into material finishes, lighting, and spatial interactions.

The following technological tools are available to architects:
- Enscape and Unity Reflect allow architects to easily convert 3D models into VR-compatible settings.

Impact:
- Enables clients to see designs in person, which enhances decision-making.
- Early problem identification lowers the need for expensive adjustments during construction.

Design Collaboration in Virtual Environments

In virtual environments, spatial computing makes it easier for stakeholders, designers, and architects to collaborate in real time.

How It Works:
- A shared 3D model allows for real-time annotation of designs, change proposals, and user interaction.
- The Wild and Arkio are two examples of tools that offer virtual places where teams may work together

to generate and enhance ideas.

Advantages:
- By successfully and early involving all stakeholders, it promotes a more inclusive design process.
- Eliminates geographical obstacles to collaboration, saving time and money.

7.2 Sales and Marketing of Real Estate

Virtual Property Tours

The use of virtual tours has revolutionized the marketing and sales of real estate by providing accessibility and ease.
- Virtual reality (VR) enables prospective buyers to view houses from a distance, saving time and money on travel.
- 360-degree video tours boost buyer confidence by providing a thorough look at every area of a home.

Technological Instruments:
- Platforms such as Matterport provide comprehensive 3D property scans, resulting in captivating and immersive virtual tours.

The effect on sales:
- Enables potential buyers to more efficiently shortlist

properties, which expedites the sales process.
- By drawing in foreign customers who would not be able to visit in person, it broadens its market reach.

AR Home Customization Tools
- Before buying a property, potential buyers can see renovations and customizations thanks to Augmented Reality.

Applications:
- AR apps let users rearrange furniture, alter wall colors, and even redesign layouts to their liking.
- Realistic AR furniture arrangement within the house is made possible by tools like IKEA Place, which assist purchasers in seeing the potential of the area.

Benefits:
- Gives customers confidence in their purchase, which improves decision-making.
- By presenting options, it lowers ambiguity and boosts customer happiness.

Improved Property Management through the Use of Spatial Computing
- Technologies related to spatial computing are also

helping property management.

Important Innovations:
- Virtual inspections are made possible by AR and VR, which streamlines maintenance and troubleshooting procedures.
- Real-time monitoring of building systems, including HVAC and electrical networks, is made possible by digital twin technology.

Impact:
- By providing predictive maintenance solutions, efficiency is increased.
- Tenant satisfaction is increased by prompt and efficient problem-solving.

7.3 Smart Cities and Urban Planning

City Planning using Digital Twins

Urban planning is revolutionized by digital twin technology, which makes it possible to create virtual versions of entire cities.

Applications:
- To evaluate the effects of different scenarios, such as population increase or infrastructure improvements,

city planners might run simulations.
- Digital twins aid in the development of more sustainable cities by offering information into environmental changes, transportation patterns, and energy consumption.
- The ability to visualize long-term effects aids in making well-informed decisions.
- Lowers the expenses related to urban development's trial-and-error methods.

AR for Designing Public Spaces

Designers are using augmented reality to make public areas more interesting and useful.

Instances:
- Before they are implemented, stakeholders can see suggested park or street plans thanks to augmented reality software.
- Members of the community can engage with AR models to offer input on suggested advancements.

Advantages:
- Promotes community involvement and makes sure that locals' needs are met in public areas.
- It expedites the approval process by giving

decision-makers lucid and captivating images.

Spatial Computing for Infrastructure and Traffic Control

- For effective traffic and infrastructure management in cities, spatial computing is essential.
- Road networks are optimized and traffic congestion is decreased with the use of digital twins for real-time traffic monitoring.
- AR systems save downtime during repairs by helping construction workers visualize subterranean utilities.
- The integration of smart technologies enhances the quality of urban infrastructure.
- By lowering traffic and enhancing general infrastructure management, cities become more livable.

Because it facilitates more effective processes, enhances decision-making, and improves user experiences, spatial computing is bringing about revolutionary change in the fields of architecture, design, and real estate. These technologies present enormous opportunities for innovation and expansion in these sectors, from producing lifelike virtual worlds to streamlining urban planning procedures. Spatial computing will surely become even more integrated in the future, opening the door to more immersive designs, smarter communities, and seamless real estate experiences.

CHAPTER 8

DEFENSE AND SECURITY APPLICATIONS OF SPATIAL COMPUTING

By facilitating effective disaster response, boosting situational awareness, and improving training techniques, spatial computing is revolutionizing military and security. These technologies transform conventional approaches to safety and protection by combining virtual reality (VR), augmented reality (AR), and data analytics to provide cutting-edge solutions for emergency, military, and security operations.

8.1 Simulation and Training for the Military

VR-Based Combat Simulations
- Military personnel can train in realistic but controlled conditions with Virtual Reality (VR) combat simulations.
- Soldiers can practice tactics and movements in

lifelike battlefields without running the danger of getting hurt in the real world.
- Various terrains and combat scenarios, including urban warfare, jungle operations, and desert missions, are replicated in virtual reality simulations.

Principal Advantages:
- Eliminates the need for travel to specialist training fields or substantial physical resources, which lowers training costs.
- By allowing soldiers to practice reactions to changing threats, such cyberattacks or drone warfare, it improves preparedness.

Technological Instruments:
- Military-grade VR training catered to particular operational requirements is offered by platforms such as VBS4 (Virtual Battlespace 4).

AR for Battlefield Awareness

By giving soldiers access to real-time, contextually relevant information, Augmented Reality (AR) is transforming battlefield awareness.

Features:
- AR headsets project vital information straight into

soldiers' fields of vision, including enemy positions, unit placements, and topographical maps.
- Microsoft's HoloLens is one example of a tool that has been modified for military usage to overlay tactical data while on operations.

Advantages:
- Reducing information latency and providing a coherent operational picture improves decision-making.
- Through shared AR interfaces that synchronize battlefield intelligence, units are better able to coordinate.

Using Spatial Computing to Maintain Equipment

Precision is necessary for maintaining intricate military equipment, and spatial computing makes these procedures easier.

How It Operates:
- AR overlays help professionals perform detailed maintenance on automobiles, airplanes, and armament systems.
- Digital twins of equipment are stored on spatial computing platforms, enabling predictive

maintenance and remote diagnostics.

Benefits:
- By facilitating quicker repairs and reducing human error, it lowers downtime.
- By giving maintenance teams current, relevant information, it improves operational efficiency.

8.2 Protection and Monitoring

Spatial Data for AI-Enhanced Surveillance

Artificial intelligence (AI) and spatial computing are revolutionizing surveillance capabilities.

Applications:
- Artificial intelligence systems examine spatial data from sensors, cameras, and drones to identify odd trends, including suspicious movements or illegal access.
- Security teams' situational awareness is enhanced by the 3D maps of monitored locations produced by spatial computing techniques.

Advantages:
- Reduces false positives, improving threat detection accuracy.

- Through real-time vulnerability identification, it facilitates preemptive responses to possible threats.

Real-World Examples:
- To control public safety and deter crime, smart cities are implementing surveillance enabled by spatial computing.

AR for Crowd Control and Law Enforcement

AR is being used by law enforcement organizations to handle challenging circumstances, including sizable crowds or dangerous operations.

Features:
- AR gadgets help officers make well-informed judgments by displaying real-time data on suspects, the environment, or possible threats.
- AR systems can assist officers in maintaining order during crowd control by guiding them through the best deployment techniques that prevent tensions from rising.

Advantages:
- By offering actionable intelligence at crucial times, it improves operational efficiency.
- By strengthening tactical preparation, it lowers the

dangers to both officers and civilians.

Operation Centers for Virtual Security

Virtual security operation centers (VSOCs) are made possible by spatial computing and allow for real-time security operations administration and monitoring.

Key Features:
- VSOCs visualize and interact with threat maps, network systems, and surveillance data using VR and AR interfaces.
- In order to coordinate reactions, security staff can work together remotely by accessing shared virtual environments.

Advantages:
- By enabling teams to oversee operations from any location, it improves flexibility.
- By combining many data streams into a single virtual interface, it improves decision-making.

8.3 Response and Recovery to Disasters

VR Disaster Scenario Training

Responders can be trained in disaster situations like

earthquakes, floods, or chemical spills using virtual reality, which offers a secure and engaging environment.

How It Operates:
- Realistic simulations are used to test trainees' capacity to react appropriately under duress.
- Challenges including managing dangerous materials, organizing evacuations, and navigating collapsed structures can all be replicated in virtual reality scenarios.

Advantages:
- By exposing responders to a range of possible crisis scenarios, it improves readiness.
- Enhances reaction speeds by imparting important decision-making abilities in a safe setting.

AR Tools for Search and Rescue Operations

By giving responders better situational awareness tools, Augmented Reality is proven to be a valuable tool in search and rescue operations.

Applications:
- AR goggles or headsets provide important data, such the whereabouts of survivors, structural flaws, or dangerous areas.

- Aerial views of catastrophe situations are provided via drone-assisted AR systems, which aid teams in planning rescue operations.

Main Benefits:
- Boosts productivity by cutting down on the amount of time required to find and help survivors.
- By seeing possible hazards before responders enter hazardous regions, safety is improved.

Spatial Computing for Emergency Assistance in Logistics

- During disaster relief efforts, effective logistics are essential, and spatial computing streamlines these procedures.
- catastrophe planners can better organize the distribution of food, water, and medical supplies by using digital twin technology, which mimics catastrophe areas.
- The best routes for transportation are determined using spatial analytics, which steer clear of hazards and impediments.

Advantages:
- Reduces bottlenecks and streamlines logistics to

expedite the provision of aid.
- By giving real-time updates on supply levels and needs, it enhances resource allocation.

The field of defense, security, and disaster management is changing as a result of spatial computing. These technologies are making systems safer and more effective, from improving surveillance with AI-driven spatial analytics to training soldiers in realistic virtual reality combat situations. The incorporation of spatial computing will become even more crucial as the industry develops, spurring innovation and guaranteeing readiness in a world that is getting more complicated by the day.

CHAPTER 9

DIFFICULTIES AND MORAL ISSUES

A number of difficulties and moral dilemmas are raised by spatial computing as it continues to transform various businesses. To guarantee that the technology is used sustainably, inclusively, and ethically, these problems must be resolved. This chapter examines the main locations where these difficulties appear and offers a thorough examination of potential solutions.

9.1 Security of Data and Privacy

Resolving Privacy Issues with AR/VR Apps
The possibility of privacy violations is one of the main issues with AR/VR technologies. These platforms frequently gather a lot of user data in order to provide experiences that are contextually aware and tailored.
Risks to Privacy:
- Sensitive data, including location, biometric

information, and user behavior patterns, may be tracked by applications.

- Constant surveillance via AR glasses or VR headsets may result in misuse or illegal data collecting.
- Implement privacy-by-design principles to ensure that user data acquisition is kept to a minimum and anonymized wherever feasible.
- User agreements must be explicit and unambiguous, explaining to users what information is gathered and how it will be used.
- Companies and regulators should make sure that data privacy laws like the CCPA and GDPR are strictly followed.

Safeguarding User Environments and Spatial Data

For spatial computing to work well, mapping user environments is essential, yet this creates opportunities for abuse.

Dangers:

- If not sufficiently secured, detailed 3D scans of residences, places of employment, or public areas may be misused.
- There could be safety issues if hackers alter spatial

data to tamper with AR/VR experiences.
- To guarantee that spatial data cannot be intercepted or altered while being transmitted, use encryption.
- To lessen vulnerability to possible breaches, use edge computing to process sensitive data locally on devices.

Use of Spatial Technology in an Ethical Way

Spatial computing has ethical ramifications that go beyond privacy to include things like manipulation and spying.

Main Concerns:
- Companies or governments may abuse AR and VR for surveillance purposes, violating people's rights.
- The development of incredibly lifelike virtual worlds may result in the dissemination of false information or deception.

Ethical Frameworks:
- Create industry-wide moral standards that regulate the application of spatial technology.
- Encourage cooperation between ethicists, technologists, and legislators in order to tackle new ethical conundrums.

9.2 Inclusivity and Accessibility

Assuring All Users Can Access AR/VR

- To provide fair participation, spatial computing systems must be usable by people with disabilities.
- The fact that many AR/VR technologies do not include accommodations for those with visual, auditory, or movement disabilities presents a challenge.
- Users with cognitive impairments may not be able to use immersive environments and complex interfaces.

Solutions:

- Create assistive technologies that enable everyone to use AR/VR devices, such haptic feedback or voice navigation.
- Incorporate functionalities such as customized controls, screen readers, and real-time captioning.

Creating Inclusive Experiences using Spatial Computing

- Beyond accessibility, inclusivity necessitates an emphasis on socioeconomic, linguistic, and cultural

diversity.
- To prevent alienating particular user groups, content creators need to take into account a variety of cultural norms and behaviors.
- Adoption of spatial computing in non-English speaking cultures may be hampered by language problems.

Strategies:
- Use AI-driven localization to modify spatial computing material for various languages and geographical areas.
- To guarantee inclusion, include a variety of user groups in the design and testing stages.

Getting Past Adoption Obstacles

Spatial computing has potential, but adoption is difficult, especially in remote or impoverished locations.

Barriers:
- Many people cannot afford the high prices of AR/VR devices.
- Spatial applications' reach is restricted by a lack of infrastructure, such as dependable internet connections.

Methods for Overcoming Obstacles:
- Fund AR/VR devices for public or educational usage in underprivileged communities.
- Create spatial applications that are offline compatible and lightweight to improve usability in low-resource environments.

9.3 Financial and Technical Obstacles

Deployment and Development Costs
- It might be difficult for smaller firms to develop and implement spatial computing solutions since they require a lot of resources.
- A significant upfront investment in software, technology, and qualified staff is one of the financial obstacles.
- Constant expenses for scalability, maintenance, and updates.

Solutions:
- Encourage collaborations among corporations, governments, and educational institutions to split expenses.
- Use open-source tools and platforms to cut down on

development costs.

Technical Restrictions in Existing Hardware for Spatial Computing

- Despite the tremendous advancements in spatial computing, hardware constraints continue to be a bottleneck.

Problems:

- The large size of many AR/VR devices makes them uncomfortable to use for extended periods of time.
- Limited processing power and battery life limit how well mobile AR/VR systems work.
- Problems with latency and connectivity can ruin real-time experiences.

Directions for the Future:

- Purchase next-generation hardware, including battery-operated, lightweight AR glasses.
- Enhance latency and real-time performance by implementing 5G and edge computing.

Techniques for Expanding Spatial Solutions

Overcoming logistical and technical obstacles is necessary to scale spatial computing technologies for widespread use.

Key Strategies:

- To make updates and customization easier, use modular designs for both software and hardware.
- Create strong development, user, and corporate ecosystems to promote adoption and innovation.
- Create standardized frameworks to guarantee that various platforms for spatial computing function together.

Unlocking spatial computing's full potential and making sure its advantages are shared fairly require addressing its difficulties and ethical issues. By putting sustainability, inclusivity, and privacy first, the sector can foster trust and open the door for ethical innovation.

CHAPTER 10

Spatial Computing's Future

Spatial computing has the potential to revolutionize human interaction with the digital and physical worlds in the future, establishing seamless integration as the standard. This chapter examines the development of spatial computing and its ramifications, from ground-breaking inventions to new business models and preparing society for broad adoption.

10.1 New Developments and Trends

Developments in Spatial Software and Hardware
- Ongoing developments in hardware and software have a significant impact on the development of spatial computing.
- Physical obstacles to entrance are being reduced by the development of compact VR headsets and lightweight, high-resolution AR glasses.

- More precise mapping and interaction with environments are made possible by improved depth sensors, LiDAR technology, and spatial cameras.
- Energy-efficient CPUs and longer battery life are making wearable technology more usable.
- Software Advancements: AI-powered algorithms are improving real-time item detection, environmental mapping, and interaction precision.
- Designing, testing, and deploying spatial apps is becoming simpler because of cross-platform development tools like Unity and Unreal Engine.
- Large-scale, cooperative experiences are becoming possible without hardware constraints thanks to cloud-based spatial computing systems.

Combining AI, 5G, and IoT with Spatial Computing

The functionality and scalability of spatial computing are being improved by its growing convergence with other revolutionary technologies.

Artificial Intelligence:
- By anticipating user requirements and actions, AI-powered systems are customizing AR/VR experiences.

- Adaptive environments that react dynamically to user inputs and environmental conditions are made possible by machine learning algorithms.

5G Networks:
- Real-time spatial experiences, like multiplayer AR games or live VR events, depend on fast, low-latency 5G connectivity.
- Spatial computing is now feasible in places with inadequate network infrastructure because of 5G's improved remote accessibility.

Internet of Things (IoT):
- IoT integration enables physical things, like industrial equipment or smart household appliances, to communicate with spatial systems.
- Advanced features like intuitive controls for home automation or real-time diagnostics for machines are made possible by the combination of IoT with AR.

Spatial Computing's Ascent in Consumer Goods

Spatial computing is rapidly being incorporated into consumer-grade devices as the technology advances.

Wearable Devices:
- AR glasses, such as those made by Nreal and Meta,

are on the verge of taking the place of conventional smartphones as the main means of digital communication.

Automotive Integration:
- AR dashboards in automobiles offer driver assistance, hazard identification, and real-time navigation.

Entertainment and Gaming:
- Spatial computing is being more widely used in entertainment because of consumer-friendly VR headsets like the Meta Quest.

10.2 Forecasts for the Upcoming Ten Years

Spatial Computing's Expanding Use in Daily Life

It is anticipated that almost every element of daily life, including work, education, leisure, and healthcare, would be impacted by spatial computing.

Education:
- Interactive AR textbooks and virtual classrooms will be commonplace resources for individualized learning.

Healthcare:

- AR-guided remote operations and VR-based immersive therapy treatments will proliferate.

Retail and E-Commerce:
- AR shopping experiences will improve customer happiness by enabling customers to see products in their spaces prior to making purchases.

Changes in the Industry and Novel Business Models
- Traditional industries will be upended by spatial computing, which will encourage the development of new ecosystems and business models.
- Similar to existing SaaS models, platforms that provide AR/VR tools, content, and services on a subscription basis will predominate.

Spatial Marketplaces:
- Users will be able to purchase, sell, or exchange virtual goods and surroundings on new online marketplaces.
- The need for UX designers, spatial data analyzers, and developers of spatial computing will increase.

The Function of Spatial Computing in the Metaverse

A key component of the future of spatial computing will be

the metaverse, a shared digital environment that combines AR, VR, and other technologies.

Key Developments:
- Persistent, interactive digital worlds that smoothly blend with the real world will be made possible by spatial computing.
- Through realistic, immersive avatars, users will traverse virtual environments for networking, working, and playing.
- The metaverse economy is expected to provide trillions of dollars in revenue by facilitating digital assets, services, and virtual real estate.

10.3 Getting Ready for a Future in Space

Developing Capabilities for the Spatial Economy

Organizations and individuals must acquire the necessary skills and abilities to prosper in a spatial future.

Important Competencies:
- Proficiency in spatial computing technologies, including WebXR, ARKit, and ARCore.
- Proficiency in game design tools, animation, and 3D modeling.

- Knowledge of how IoT, 5G, and AI are integrated into ecosystems for spatial computing.

Initiatives in Education:
- Specialized courses covering both technical and creative aspects of spatial computing should be offered by universities and training facilities.
- Upskilling staff to operate AR/VR equipment should be the main goal of corporate training initiatives.

Opportunities for Investing in Spatial Technologies

The revolution in spatial computing is mostly being driven by investors.

The following are promising areas for investment:
- startups creating cutting-edge AR/VR software or hardware.
- Businesses that specialize in creating spatial material, like virtual production or immersive gaming.
- Cloud computing solutions and 5G networks are examples of infrastructure developments.
- The adoption of spatial computing can be accelerated by partnerships between governments, educational institutions, and technological

companies.

Promoting Multidisciplinary Cooperation

- Across businesses and disciplines, cooperation is essential to the success of spatial computing.
- To create user-friendly spatial experiences, technologists, designers, and content producers must collaborate.
- Guidance from ethicists and policymakers is necessary to guarantee the egalitarian and responsible use of spatial computing.

The following are some advantages of collaboration:

- Diverse viewpoints and expertise can promote innovation.
- Taking a comprehensive approach to solving societal, technological, and ethical issues.

The digital and physical worlds are about to undergo significant change as a result of spatial computing, which will influence how we interact, live, and work. Society can fully realize its potential to build an inventive, inclusive, and immersive future by staying ahead of new trends, tackling obstacles, and encouraging cooperation.

ABOUT THE AUTHOR

 Author and thought leader in the IT field Taylor Royce is well known. He has a two-decade career and is an expert at tech trend analysis and forecasting, which enables a wide audience to understand complicated concepts.

Royce's considerable involvement in the IT industry stemmed from his passion with technology, which he developed during his computer science studies. He has extensive knowledge of the industry because of his experience in both software development and strategic consulting.

Known for his research and lucidity, he has written multiple best-selling books and contributed to esteemed tech periodicals. Translations of Royce's books throughout the world demonstrate his impact.

Royce is a well-known authority on emerging technologies and their effects on society, frequently requested as a speaker at international conferences and as a guest on tech podcasts. He promotes the development of ethical technology, emphasizing problems like data privacy and the digital divide.

In addition, with a focus on sustainable industry growth, Royce mentors upcoming tech experts and supports IT education projects. Taylor Royce is well known for his ability to combine analytical thinking with technical know-how. He sees a time when technology will ethically benefit humanity.

www.ingramcontent.com/pod-product-compliance
Lightning Source LLC
Chambersburg PA
CBHW050325230526
45471CB00005B/2362